WHEN THE BELOVED CALLS

SUJATA AMEYA

Envision Earth Media

WHEN THE BELOVED CALLS
By Sujata Ameya

Mandalas and sketches by Sujata Ameya
Cover design and page layout by Nivriti Roddam

First published in paperback in 2019 by Envision Earth Media
A division of The Open Circle LLC, USA
Copyright © Sujata Ameya 2019

Sujata Ameya asserts the moral right to be identified as the author of this work.

www.inner-horizons.com Email:ameyasujata@gmail.com
https://www.linkedin.com/in/sujatapotay
http://facebook.com/ArtandScienceofSelfActualization
https://www.facebook.com/Art-Science-of-The-Be-Loved-147200285805978/

The views and opinions expressed in this book are the author's own and the facts are as reported by her, and the publishers are not in any way liable for the same.
All rights reserved. No part of this publication may be reduced, stored in a retrieval system, or transmitted, in any form or by any means, electronic, mechanical, photocopying, recording or otherwise, without the prior permission of the publishers.

ISBN: 978-1-7330838-1-2
Price: US $21.49

Envision EarthMedia,
A division of The Open Circle LLC, 902 Gribbin Ln 3B,
Toledo OH 43612, USA.
www.envisionearthmedia.com

"Sujata Ameya's luminous and mesmerizing collection *When the Beloved Calls* is poetry of the mysterious and the sacred, an exquisite wonder that beckons us to her 'cosmos within' and 'many-splendoured grace' so we can experience the redemptive power of love."

Hélène Cardona, internationally acclaimed poet, actor and translator
www.helenecardona.com

"A wonderful book of poems on love. These are perfect to be savoured over a year, one poem a week!"

Subhash Kak, Scientist, Mathematician, Indologist, Regents Professor, Oklahoma State University, Author of *The Loom of Time, Mind and Self*, and others

"Sujata's poems belong to the lineage of Bhakti poets like Mira, whose longing is intense, and is about awakening to one's self in relationship with the Beloved. They are also reminiscent of the Biblical *Song of Solomon* as well as Sufi songs that epitomise deep yearning for the ultimate union with the Divine Other. Some poems carry the voice of a woman's realisation of her own power. A flash of profound self-recognition is seen in others."

Neela Bhattacharya Saxena,
Author of *Absent Mother God of the West*

"Reading your poems has left me in a space that is hard to put in words. I am alone, and I can hear many voices speak to me. Some are soaked with longing, some are joyous, some are melancholic, some are seeking healing, some offering healing, some saying 'Just see me as I am,' and some saying 'Will you love me still if you see?.' The space was soft and quiet, it did not echo anything back. It just held the voices. I quickly realised that The Beloved is there with us all the time, but we seem to yearn for it as though it is not, and recognise it only in spaces that are soft and quiet. Thank you for taking me there. I am very grateful to you for having shared these poems with me. They have a quality of passion seen through the lens of dispassion. May be that's when compassion grows. I am sure many readers will find themselves resonating with you, having conversations with themselves and perhaps with you."

Raghu Ananthanarayanan,
Author of *Totally Aligned Organization* and *Leadership Dharma*;
Co-Founder, Flame TAO Knoware

"Sujata's poems are refreshing and convey genuine and deep feelings. They are very moving, thought-provoking, exploring the meaning of love, the positives of waiting, contradictions and adapting. I thoroughly enjoyed reading them! I feel drawn to go back to them from time to time."

Gurumani Vaiyacheri, Former Country Director, India,
Project Concern International

"The poems reminded me of Meera and her love towards her beloved Krishna."
Nagesh Kumar Battula, Managing Director, FHD Group and Organo

"A heart-warming set of poems capturing a resplendent gamut of emotions—all associated with love!"

Raj Raghunathan, Professor of Marketing, University of Texas, Austin,
Author of *If You're So Smart, Why Aren't You Happy?*

WHEN THE BELOVED CALLS

"I've been reading your poems over and over again, trying to find the right words to express how I feel about your writing. After all, it's not every day that one comes across such brilliance that it ignites one's imagination and captivates the mind so spellbindingly. It's been really long since I read poetry as magical as 'The Beloved.' It touched the inner recesses of my soul and echoed my feelings too, in an inexplicable way. You're truly gifted, my friend. If you don't share your writings with the world, you'll be depriving the readers of the deep pleasure I experienced. And that, according to me, would be unfair. It was akin to a thirst being quenched as I read line after line, poem after poem. Thank you for sharing them with me. I'm honoured."

Vanaja Banagiri, Regional Editor, Ritz Media Group;
Author of *Butterflies and Barbed Wires*

"Reading your poems, at times, left me with the feeling that I was reading a translation of our ancient Sanskrit sacred texts that talk about love, devotion and surrender to the Divine. It is rich fare that I will keep going back to."

Narendran K.S., Author of *Life After MH370: Journeying Through a Void*, Principal Consultant, FLAME TAO Knoware

"I read your poems – most of them several times. I love the wisdom. I love the depth. I loved that your poems force us to think. And you certainly have a way with words. There are many nuggets of gold in your poems about The Beloved who can be God, Mother Nature, lover/partner/husband, a child, and also your own self."

Katia Novet Saint-Lot, Writer, Mother, Traveller and Author of *Amadi's Snowman*

"I just read your collection of The Beloved poems and am reeling from your outpourings!! What a 'pravaha' (flow) of pellucid heart-tugging odes to the Beloved within, without any punctuations to block the flow. The state of bhava, (feeling) and the rasa of bhakti (dedication and devotion) to the adorable Beloved – that you have channelled through your own anubhava (experience) – can be read at the level of Krishna-prema (love and pining), as a call to the inner Beloved, the atma (soul) within, and as soul-stirring love songs to one's life-partner. The poem on Awareness is pure Vedanta! Your poems touch the soul and move the heart through their entrancing Calls to the Beloved at so many levels."

Kumar S. Sharma, Ph.D., Author of *Age of Ananda – Conscious Evolution to the Life Divine*

"I read your poems, not once but twice. Some I read many times as they struck a very deep chord within. I'd say this collection is an essential reading for every man and woman, whether or not in a relationship, to get a taste of love and longing, and to understand the uplifting potential of vulnerability."

Sanjay Darbha, Founder and CEO, PeerLend

"In these poems, Sujata takes us through a mesmerising deep-dive into the nature of The Beloved. She paints with a dazzling palette that pushes us to simultaneously consider phenomena like Longing, Wonder, Immersion, Play, Awareness, Seeking, Desire, Restoration and much, much more. Her ability to be unpretentious and to yet leave the reader with a sense of deep touch is remarkable. Don't be surprised if you are left with an ache in your heart after reading this book!"

Kartikeyan, V., Chief Consultant, Vistas Consulting,
Co-Author of *Discover the Alchemist Within*

CONTENTS

	Dedication	vii
	Foreword	viii
	Preface	x
	Acknowledgements	xii
	Prologue	xv
	Epilogue	88

WHEN THE BELOVED CALLS

1	Communion	2
2	Remembrance	3
3	Together	5
4	Questing	6
5	Swirling	7
6	Solitude	9
7	Homecoming	10
8	Yearning	13
9	The Cosmos Within	14
10	Freedom	15
11	Nameless	17
12	Grace	18
13	Waiting	19
14	Embrace	21
15	Perennial	22
16	Release	23
17	The Path	25
18	Sanctuary	26
19	Benediction	27
20	Twinflame	29
21	Hope	30
22	Gratitude	31
23	Wherever	33
24	Journey	34
25	Faith	35
26	Recognition	37
27	Only You	38
28	Soulmate	39

CONTENTS (CONTINUED)

29	Miracle	41
30	Solace	42
31	Merging	43
32	Desire	44
33	Alone	46
34	Flicker	47
35	Meeting	48
36	Echo	50
37	The Veil	51
38	Rejuvenation	52
39	Healing	54
40	Seeking	55
41	Promise	56
42	Reflection	57
43	Kindred Spirit	59
44	North Star	60
45	Awareness	61
46	Immersion	62
47	With Me	63
48	Magic Mirror	64
49	Longing	67
50	Grief	68
51	Wholeness	70
52	Restoration	71
53	Distance	72
54	Reckoning	73
55	Unbroken	74
56	Play	75
57	Swing	76
58	Initiation	78
59	Privilege	79
60	Everything	80
61	Preciousness	82
62	Melting	83
63	Wonder	84
64	Unfolding	85

Dedicated to

The Beloved of the Universe
JAGAD-GURU SHRI KRISHNA

And

My Beloved here on Earth

KALYANA-MITRA SAKHA

The source of my power and
The purpose of my path
But for whom
These poems wouldn't exist

FOREWORD

They say we must pay attention to the context to understand its content. Yesterday, 15 December, 2018, I watched a sublime performance on the life and poetry of Andal, the 8th Century girl/poet/goddess of South India, and came home awash in the intense love for the Divine Beloved that she still transmits to us across time and space. I am enthralled at the devotional mystical tradition of women poet-saints of India, through the ages, who have kept this land, nay the planet, soaked in showers and rivers of love and grace. Mira Bai, Lal Ded, Akka Mahadevi... so many before them and after them.

Today, 16 December, 2018, is the sixth anniversary of the horrific gang-rape of a young girl, on a moving bus in Delhi. Such was the brutality with which Nirbhaya was mutilated that she succumbed to her internal injuries, a few days later. The event sent shock-waves through the Nation and the world. It was as if every woman was raped awake.

Since that fateful day of 16 December, 2012, I have wondered deeply about Man's impulse to terrorise, violate and destroy. I discovered it has its roots in a drive in our Human body, called *thanatos*, hard-wired into our biology for our survival, from the time of our evolution out of the animal kingdom. (Not) Surprisingly, it is the same root from which *eros*, the sexual drive for procreation arises. Together, they are the Vital, the life-force needed to perpetuate Life. We cannot suppress one without suppressing or distorting the other. And we cannot do without either.

'The weak flesh' has been the bane of religious paths the world over, as this powerful instinctual drive overpowers Man's quest for transcending 'impure' carnal needs, in order to attain 'pure' spiritual heights and true bliss. *Soma* and *psyche*, Body and Soul have been as if in a savage struggle for dominance over Man.

Until, through Time, mystics have discovered a Radical Path. The path of The Beloved. To seek the Divine as the object of one's desire. To turn the inevitable presence of the erotic impulse to fuel the tremendous intensity and energy needed to tear the 'veil of separation.' To attain the spiritual breakthrough and experience the true ground of our Being, our true Nature, our *interbeing*, our Oneness. That there is no 'other.'

They have gone on to discover that indeed, this ground of Being, is *Ananda*. Love, Peace, Joy, indescribable. Many simply stay there, tripping over in Bliss. A rare few, thankfully, return to light the path for the rest of us who may have an appetite, nay, a longing to taste what they are tasting, drink what they are drinking.

Sujata Ameya is one such way-shower. A true yogini, whose everyday outer life belies the splendour of her *queendom* within. She has quested and yearned, wrestled and submitted, and turned every corner on the pathless path, thankfully stopping to record the inspired experiences, on the way, for us to learn from and savour. And, if so graced, to be initiated by.

I felt loved by each of Sujata's poems here. How could I not? Each is a sacred fruit of her Beloved's *deeksha*. And since that which is deeply personal is also deeply Universal, I found myself particularly resonating with these poems: *Waiting, Journey* and *The Cosmos Within*; and was enthralled by *Longing, Awareness, Kindred Spirit*, and *Grief*. I feel humbled and grateful, and in complete awe at the depth of her being reflected in her poems.

I would encourage our dear reader to read the book fully; and then return time and again, to open the book randomly, with an intention to get succour or to drink from the well, and to feel reconnected with their Beloved. I am sure each poem will remain as a living rasa. Never going stale.

There is a word in Sanskrit, *rasa-anubhava*. It means 'savouring the juice of an experience.' An experience that quenches our deepest thirst. The ultimate thirst underlying all desires. May Sujata's labour of love, birthed as each twinkling diamond-droplet of a poem, go a long way in quenching our thirst. And may the world be a safer, more rapturous and awe-filled place for it.

Thank you for sharing your soul with us, Sujata.

Nilima Bhat
Founder-Director, Shakti Fellowship;
Co-author, *Shakti Leadership* and *My Cancer Is Me*
Mumbai
16th December, 2018

PREFACE

The idea of a profound and transformational friendship between two individuals is perhaps as old as the human species itself. Most ancient indigenous cultures have one or more specific words, or a phrase in their language, to refer to this uniquely human experience of a close/caring bond, a relationship that is experienced as special and uplifting.

In the Celtic tradition there is the idea of a soul-friend, 'Anam Cara.' 'Anam' is the Gaelic word for soul and 'Cara' is the word for friend. With the 'Anam Cara,' you could share your innermost self, your mind and your heart. The friendship with your Anam Cara cuts across all convention, morality, and category, beyond the limitations of space and time. It is about a love that evoked trust and belonging because it could read the secret signature of your individuality and recognise your sacred identity. You feel joined in love in an ancient and eternal way with this 'friend of your soul.'

In the Indian (Hindu) tradition, this special bond between friends and lovers is referred to as 'sakha-pan.' 'Sakha' in Sanskrit means 'close friend' and 'pan' means 'ness' as in 'sweet-ness,' or 'ship' as in 'friend-ship.' Perhaps, the most well-known sakha-pan is the one between the 'divine couple' Shri Krishna and Radha, which has for centuries, captured the imagination of lovers, friends and poets alike. Another Sanskrit term, used to refer to the devotion and bond between a deity and devotee as well as that between humans, is 'Atma-bandhu,' a 'kindred soul' ('atma' meaning 'soul' and 'bandhu' meaning 'kin'). The friendship between Shri Ram and Hanuman is the best example of this 'devotion to each other' ('Bhakti' in Sanskrit).

In Christianity, 'soulmate' and 'beloved' refer to the deepest and most special of friendships. A soulmate is a friend who finishes all of your sentences, or the one you can have a full conversation with, using no words at all, or the one who is willing to risk his life for you. These references from the Old Testament capture the sentiment very well: "Happy is the one who can say from the heart, this is my beloved, and this is my friend" (*Song of Solomon* 5:16); "I have found the one whom my soul loves" (*Song of Solomon* 3:4), and "A sweet friendship refreshes the soul (Proverbs 27:9).

In Judaism, the concept of a soulmate ('Beshert' – which also means 'inevitable' or 'preordained') has its roots in the *Talmud*. The *Talmud* is the compilation of the historic rabbis 'discussing' or 'debating' the tenets of the Hebrew Bible of the Jews, *Torah*. The idea of 'Beshert' is that soulmates are actually two parts of the same whole, who have been temporarily separated by Divine Providence, and are searching/longing to unite with their missing counterparts. While the Jews place great emphasis on free will and right action, the romantic notion of searching for and finding 'the one' who is divinely destined as your life-partner, is very popular and practised with enthusiasm and faith.

The Buddhist tradition also has the concept of the 'Kalyana-mitra,' the 'noble-friend' – a friend who cares for your well-being and is committed to support you in living your life honourably, and to guide you in actualizing your unique purpose. The Kalyana-mitra, will not accept pretensions, but will gently and very firmly confront you with your doings and failings. The Kalyana-mitra complements your vision in a kind and critical way.

The Sufis speak of a mystical path of love in which God, or Truth, is experienced as the Beloved, where the inner relationship of the lover and Beloved takes the seeker to oneness with God. This *unio mystica* happens within the heart, where the lover and Beloved unite in love's ecstasy. On this path, the seeker ecstatically calls the Beloved by any of the 99 names of the One, each name an elevating description of the glorious attributes of the Divine. The only obstacle that keeps the seeker from experiencing the Beloved is his ego i.e. his own personal identity, which he experiences as separate from God. The eleventh-century Sufi, Ansârî, expressed this very simply: "When you learn to lose yourself, you will meet the Beloved. There is no other secret to be learnt."

I am certain there are more such examples from other traditions. As John O'Donohue says, "**One of the deepest longings of the human soul is the longing to be seen.**" Unfortunately, there is no mirror in the world where you can catch a glimpse of your soul. No one can see his life totally. As there is a blind-spot in the retina of the human eye, there is also in the soul a blind side that you are not able to see. Therefore, you must depend on the one you love to see of you what you cannot see for yourself. The one you love, your 'Anam Cara,' your 'Kalyana-Mitra,' becomes the truest mirror to reflect your soul. Such friendship is creative and critical; it is willing to negotiate awkward and uneven territories of contradiction and woundedness. The honesty and clarity of true friendship also brings out the real contour of your spirit. It is beautiful to have such a presence in your life."

Sujata Ameya
Hyderabad, India
1st January, 2019

ACKNOWLEDGEMENTS

This book has been brought to fruition with the loving help, support and presence of beings, human and divine. I would like to express my heartfelt gratitude to:

The Divine Mother Lalita Devi, for choosing me to be the channel for this labour of love, for painting my path with this ethereal landscape, and hand-holding me always. I am grateful to simply be alive, and I look forward to the rest of this journey with curiosity and anticipation.

Shri. Sai Baba of Shirdi, for answering in this delightful way my life-long quest and unconscious prayer: "I want to know what love is." It turns out that love is an unending dance with your soul while you gaze into the eyes of your Beloved. Love is an ongoing adventure of self-discovery.

My mother Smt. Lalita Bai Patil and father Shri. Hanumanth Rao Patil, whose implicit faith, unquestioned acceptance and continuous blessings I have always taken for granted, like the air I breathe. No matter what I do or fail to do, their love remains constant. If I can claim to know the taste of unconditional love, it is because of them.

My maternal uncle, Dr. Manohar Shinde, for his undisguised pride and unalloyed adoration, for insisting and always encouraging me to claim my place in the stars.

All my clients, students and workshop participants, whose unabashed sharing of their personal stories of living, loving and longing, has greatly enriched my own understanding and experience of it all.

Prabhath P., of Envision Earth Media, for his kind words and honest appreciation, for seeing value in my poems and persuading me to consider publishing them. And most importantly, for his gentle and sensitive editing. Alex Moyer of Envision Earth Media, for offering to publish this collection of poems.

Nilima Bhat, for reading through the poems at heart-speed and writing such a thoughtful, generous and beautiful foreword.

Vijay Bhat, for his incisive observations, critical questions and helpful suggestions about all aspects of the writing and publishing of this book.

The many wise and kind-hearted well-wishers, for taking the trouble to read all the poems, in advance, sharing their authentic feedback and giving liberal endorsements for the book: Hélène Cardona, Dr. Subhash Kak, Raghu Ananthanarayanan, Dr. Kumar S. Sharma, Neela Bhattacharya-Saxena, Narendran K.S., Katia Novet Saint-Lot, Raj Raghunathan, Gurumani Vaiyacheri, Nagesh Kumar Battula, Vanaja Banagiri, Kartikeyan V. and Sanjay Darbha.

Nivriti Roddam for her patience and creativity in designing the covers and the layout of the book. Sudha Mehta, for her suggestions regarding punctuation and sequencing.

My friends on Facebook, many of whom I have never met, for their generous appreciation, enquiry and encouragement, whenever I posted these poems.

My Soul-brothers: Dr. Donald Pilch (Uncle Don), C.V.L. Narasimha Murthy, J. S. Murthy, Amit Taggarse, Sunil Deshmukh, Vivek Shinde, and Balasubramanian Iyer, for their respect, support and encouragement.

My Shakti sorority, for their unstinted caring, championing, cautioning and cheer-leading: Swati (Sivanagakumari Boggavarapu), Amala Akkineni, Jayashree Murthy, Jaya Arun, Rahi Santhanam, Dr. Vasuprada Kartic, Dr. Swapna Narendra, Dr. Kiran Krishnamurti, Meera Marthi, Manisha Nair, Dr. Kausar Shaik, Shanthi Balasubramanian, Kalyani Krishnan, Malavika Raghuram, Afroze Fatima, Sudha Prakash, Aparna Bidarkar, Kavita Deshmukh, Monica Gupta, and several others that I may have missed mentioning here, and who I hope will forgive the oversight.

My sister Sangeeta Patil, for her extraordinary love and her skilful multitasking between grocery-shopping, shoulder-lending, babysitting, house-keeping, counselling, feeding or pampering. She has mastered the art of holding her own yearning in one hand and nurturing the world with the other. Without her ever-ready availability and support, I wouldn't have had the luxury of the undisturbed solitude that I so often need and crave.

My late brother Pratap Patil, who although few years younger to me, foresaw my gift of healing years before I could see it myself, and declared that I would light the path for many. Having lived only 30 summers, his unusual wisdom, humility, compassion , generosity and love remain in the hearts of every person who knew him.

My daughters Anushka and Ananya, for their independent spirit, spontaneous mischief and unstoppable laughter; their matter-of-fact acceptance and instant forgiving of my moods and methods, and their silent pride and adoration of their 'manic mom.' They are the double jackpot of my life, my daily supply of unconditional love.

My past: The person I was married to, for his utmost sincerity, commitment and support, for being exactly who he was and was not. My former self, for her incredible poverty of consciousness, confounded by her sheer tenacity. Our marriage, for unfolding precisely the way it did and did not.

Over time, these three unique ingredients together, created the exact circumstances needed to dry up and harden my heart until it eventually cracked. Looking back at it all today, I am grateful that it did. For it is through those cracks that love could make its way back in again. Love bereft of the colour and chorus of centuries of conditioning. Love shorn of titles and entitlement. Love without tags, roles and expectations. Love stripped of all epithets and adjectives. Love that simply IS. It is this **love, immeasurable and magnanimous – AMEYA –** that finally healed my heart, made it whole and rendered it aglow from within.

And last but not the least, I am eternally grateful to my Beloved Sakha, for awakening me to the panorama of love within and without, and for quietly rejoicing in my ecstasy.

Sujata Ameya
Hyderabad, India
1st January, 2019

PROLOGUE

"Falling in love you remain a child, rising in love you mature. By and by love becomes not a relationship, rather it becomes a state of your being. Not that you are in love – now, you are love." **- Osho**

When the Beloved calls, you respond in the only way possible: with Reverence and Wonder.

The poems in this collection are inspired by and dedicated to the Beloved within each of us, the ancient and eternal soulmate, the doorway to wisdom and grace.

I must admit that these poems literally 'came to me' while I was struggling hard to comprehend and explain to myself a surreal experience that had possessed me. As I began to pen them down, the poems helped me dive deep into, and truly savour the richness, of a kind of love that I had not experienced before, a love that defies description.

As I sincerely wrote them down, these poems revealed to me the sublime and transformative power of ordinary love when it is unfettered by labels, frameworks and expectations, yet a love that is real and palpable, and as abiding as one's breath.

Love that does not seek your permission to touch you, love that compels you to yield.

Love that transports you to a higher dimension, love that immerses you in sweet surrender.

Love that invokes the warrior in you, to honour and protect itself, even at the cost of its own fulfilment.

Love that resuscitates your soul and revitalises your spirit, regardless of, or in spite of, your story so far.

Love that evokes a delicate faith that allows the love to flow without directing it, faith that you never knew existed within you.

Love that kindles a fierce and enduring care for another, such that you reckon your own worth and begin to value yourself.

Love that heals, redeems and restores everything in you that has been refused and reduced by the vagaries inherent in the unfolding of life.

Love that melts your ego-identity, overrides your strongest beliefs and redefines the meaning of devotion and worship.

Love that beckons you to plunge into uncertainty and explore unknown destinations.

And you concede, disregarding the cries of fear and doubt inside you. You follow, ignoring the persistent 'what if's.

You agree to walk a path, confusing to the mind, but enticing to the heart, for it is a path laid by your soul, which can be lit only by the free-will of your spirit.

This collection of poems is an offering of love, to love, by love and for love. May you be touched and moved by its tender power. May you meet and abide with your Beloved within, for always!

Sujata Ameya
Hyderabad, India
1st January, 2019

WHEN THE BELOVED CALLS

COMMUNION

Speak to me my Beloved
Just as I speak to you
Unabashedly, never holding
Back a tear nor hiding a fear
Speak to me my Beloved
Just as I speak to you
Of the journeys of my soul
And the longings of my heart
Speak to me my Beloved
Just as I speak to you
For between our speaking and
Our listening, flows the river
Of eternal truth from which
We may both sip the nectar
Of communion slow and sweet.

REMEMBRANCE

Do you know my Beloved
That from seasons far away
Very often I remember
The warmth of your embrace
That swiftly elevates my soul
Do you know my Beloved
That from galaxies far away
Very often I recognise
The waft of your presence
That pervades my existence.

WHEN THE BELOVED CALLS

TOGETHER

Do not rush to name
A destination my Beloved
Do not hasten your steps
Nor hurry on this path
Walk close to me slowly
In silence so that love can
Keep pace with our strides
For you must know my Beloved
That love is an unceasing
Song of my spirit
That I can hear and sing
Only when my heart beats
In rhythm with yours
For you must know my Beloved
That love is an unending
Dance of my soul
That I can see and partake
Only when I gaze long
Into your lucid lotus eyes.

QUESTING

You may not my Beloved
Yet know what you seek
Unless you let your heart
Wander on paths untrod
Unknown to the all-knowing
Sceptic who feels in fact
Torn between the tugging
In opposite directions
Of your hope on one hand
And your fear on the other
Now is the time my Beloved
To ask your guide within
To steer your heart to venture
Into territories uncharted
To nudge it gently to dabble
In the art of walking lightly
While burning in your quest
Until you see that you actually
Become that which you seek
But dimly, slowly and quietly.

SWIRLING

When I can my Beloved
No longer contain
The ecstasy surging forth
From the centre of my being
When I am bewildered
As the ecstasy gives way
All of a sudden unbidden
To a gushing fountain
Of anguish uncertain
Springing from a depth
I often fail to fathom
When I can my Beloved
No longer stretch my arms
To hold this swirling
Within my inner world
Then I recall the comfort
Of your steady embrace
And so yearn to behold
Your calm sparkling eyes.

SOLITUDE

In your absence my Beloved
I am immersed in long days
Of blissful selflessness and
Nights of utter self-absorption
Then there are times when
The breeze of the mundane
Wafts stealthily through a small
Crevice in my sweet solitude
Disrupting my rapture and
Stirring ripples of sweet longing
Even though my heart beats
Always in rhythm with yours.

HOMECOMING

And then my Beloved
When you become weary
Of the relentless pursuit
Of self-improvement, fuelled
By self-denial and self-rejection

When you become weary
Of the relentless pursuit
Of transformation, driven
By brazen self-abandonment

When you become weary
Of the relentless pursuit
Of loving and accepting
Yourself, alternating with
Self-loathing and self-berating

When you become weary
Of the relentless pursuit
Of becoming bigger and more
Wanting to transcend what is
Chasing what is not or yet to be
And landing right back in
The exact same moment that
You perpetually turn away from

When you become weary
Of the relentless pursuit
Of perfecting your Being
Which has always and ever
Been already perfect, except
In the minds of those with
Impaired vision and imperfect eyes

When you are exhausted from
The pointlessness of pursuing
Perfection beyond here and now
Remember my Beloved there is
Forever a place dedicated to you
In a quiet corner of my heart
Where you can do no wrong.

YEARNING

At long last my Beloved
Just when we were to meet
While I was anticipating
Myriad star-bursts of delight
Just then the tide turned
And the clouds darkened
To block your way with
Fierce lightning and thunder
I wait for you my Beloved
In the hope that the torrent
Will soon cease and reveal
To you the path to my heart.

THE COSMOS WITHIN

In your presence I learnt my Beloved
Disguised in the giving is the receiving
Chanting your name is meditation and
In feeding you my soul is nourished

Inviting you fills my heart with warmth
Waiting for you my patience is revealed
Remembering you nurtures my faith and
In longing for you my hope is redeemed

Deep in the lines of the palms of your hands
I see my path to myriad journeys within
In the oceanic depth of your sparkling eyes
I fathom wisdom and ecstasy hidden in me

Mesmerised by the trail of your footprints
I discover the intricacy of existence itself
In following the rhythm of your breathing
I quiver as the cosmos pulses through me

In seeking to embrace you fully I begin to
Reckon the unfathomable expanse of my soul
In listening intently to the beat of your heart
I hear the ecstatic swirling of galaxies galore

Beholding your handsome face I glimpse
What glory and splendour it is to be me
In the soft lines around your smile I read
The raptures we've shared through eternity.

FREEDOM

In pursuit of your being
In the search for my soul
My Beloved I have been
Adrift for way too long
Grant me the confines
Of your arms so I may
Come alive and thrive
Or perhaps find at last
The solace and freedom
In your embrace to die.

NAMELESS

When the soul feels healed
By unexpected compassion
When the being feels restored
By a fortuitous touch of love
Then the mind feels compelled
To stretch and wrap itself
Around the experience, the ego
Feels obliged to give it a name
But what name shall I give to
You my precious my Beloved
For you are to me invaluable
Your presence unfathomable
Your touch indescribable
To me you are the channel
As well as the Source itself
Of love serene and grace divine.

GRACE

As you harden up trying
Very hard not to break
That brittle surface is indeed
What's required for Grace
To deal a swift blow that
Lights you up from within
So that through those very
Cracks your unique brilliance
May burst forth and shine.

WAITING

I thank you my Beloved for
Not coming when I called
For making me wait long
Nights of loneliness and
For making me weep
Tears of deep sorrow
Until they dried into
Parched days of despair
Yet gazing unmoving
At your path has steadied
My oft wavering hope
And listening intently
To the whisper of every
Breeze has sharpened
My blunted intuition
Holding very close these
Pangs of yearning has
Made strong and large
My rather feeble heart
It seems my Beloved that
My anguished longing has
Slowly resolutely melted
Into love tender and sweet
That is enough and more
For you and me for eternity.

EMBRACE

Do you know my Beloved
That every night I fall
Asleep to the calming rhythm
Of your breath, and the sweet
Lullaby of your heartbeat
Do you know my Beloved
That every morning I wake
Enveloped in your arms
Beholding your gentle face
And your sparkling lotus eyes
Do you know my Beloved
That over seasons short and long
You may not be next to me but
My heart dances to your song.

PERENNIAL

You must know my Beloved
Your presence is elemental
To my journey my very being
To my growing my becoming
When I wallow you chide me
Like fire cleansing ruthlessly
All that is old dead and futile
When I speak you hold me
Like the earth holding quietly
All that is true false or ugly
When I yearn you behold me
Like water quenching gently
All that is parched and buried
When I dare you uphold me
Like the air elevating swiftly
All that is right true and lofty
When I walk you guide me
Like the sky lighting steadily
My path to infinite possibilities.

RELEASE

Hear my plea my Beloved
Even as I am stung by pangs
Of loneliness unconsoled
That has frozen my heart
Even as I am impaled by shards
Of longing that I ruthlessly ignore
My eyes are parched with
Unshed tears of many years
So hold me close my Beloved
Long enough so that I can sigh
And behold me so my Beloved
Long enough that I can cry.

THE PATH

Purpose and Meaning may be
Two sides of the same coin
Purpose is revealed in why I live
Meaning is experienced in how I live
Purpose is where I meet the without
Meaning is when I meet the within
Purpose is what I do in your world
Meaning is how I feel in my world
Purpose is driven by grit whereas
Meaning is enlivened by grace
When Meaning becomes lost
Purpose too loses its punch
When Meaning is re-discovered
Purpose finds its purpose again
Meaning is dynamic like a river
Ever-fresh, exploring, finding a path.
Purpose like the banks firmly holds
Shapes and directs its eternal flow
As Meaning evolves and clarifies
Purpose unfolds and manifests.

SANCTUARY

Do you know my Beloved
That my mind conjures
Alluring tales, compelling
Dreams and countless ideas
That my hands then deftly
Craft and I proudly display
To marvelling crowds
Spellbound by the engrossing mix
Of labour and love but
They know not my Beloved
That the sweet secret behind
This enchanting skillfulness
Is the mesmerising melody
Of your precious heartbeat
That quietly shadows mine
You must know then
For sure my Beloved that
I may blend everywhere yet
Belong really nowhere except
In the sanctuary of your heart.

BENEDICTION

For each and every real
And imagined deprivation
There is a benediction
Sometimes apparent but
Most often disguised
Hidden well and deep
Within the very adversity
For you to discover on your
Own or sometimes, quietly
Delivered by a kindred soul
With an unforeseen hand
Of pristine love and grace.

TWINFLAME

Why do I so long
For you my Beloved
I feel seen when
I See you my Beloved
My spirit is lit when you
Touch me my Beloved
I feel heard when
I Hear you my Beloved
I feel cherished when
I Hold you my Beloved
My soul delights when I
Behold you my Beloved.

HOPE

Do you know my Beloved
That in the unseen depths
Of my soul my very being
Flows an undying stream
Of grief intense unrelenting
Do you know my Beloved
That it is only the chanting
Unbroken unceasing of your
Sweet name that keeps ajar
The leaden door of my heart
That has for long been intent
On shutting wholly, shattered by
The illusion that is this world.

GRATITUDE

Gratitude my Beloved
For your pristine presence
So that I could
Come into my own
Gratitude my Beloved
For your conscious being
So that I could find my
Playful divinity within
Gratitude my Beloved
For your sweet friendship
So that I could befriend
My Goddess Radha within
Gratitude my Beloved
For skillfully doing nothing
So that I could reconnect
With my Krishna within.

WHEREVER

It does not matter my Beloved
Whether you are near or far
Each day in your arms I wake
To behold your delightful face
It does not matter my Beloved
Whether you are here or there
For your pristine stillness reflects
To me my many-splendoured grace
It does not matter my Beloved
Whether you are away or close
For who renders it resplendent
Undoubtedly my heart knows.

JOURNEY

And then my Beloved
As my mind wandered wide and far
Across the barren landscape
Of my life, of my many journeys
Down the deep valley of longing and
Into the dense forest of heartbreak
Up the steep mountain of persistence
Plodding vast plains of not knowing
Through the desert of dry despair
But emerged actually drenched
By unexpected showers of Grace
Startled awake from unconsciousness
By a downpour of divine beneficence
Then it struck me my Beloved
That my heart had to break
Open to receive your love
That I was being prepared
To welcome you in fullness
And to meet you in wholeness.

FAITH

I came to meet you there
My Beloved, in the distant
Realm of sheer possibility
With quiet trepidation
And utter uncertainty
I didn't know then
How long it would take or
how long I would have to wait
To behold your beautiful face
To dance in your adoring gaze
To soak in your handsomeness
To exhale in your embrace
To bask in your warmth
To tremble in your admiration
To come alive in your attention
To shine in your brilliance
Breath comes easy my Beloved
Now that we finally met.

RECOGNITION

The river lashes wildly at the hill
Lamenting that he blocks her way
Until she sees that he holds and
Contains both her fury and play
The hill bemoans that he cannot
Move like the river until he sees
Deep in her every crest and trough
That he too moves with her waves.

ONLY YOU

No matter when I look
In the mirror my Beloved
I see you and only you
I long to meet you and
Gaze into your eyes
So that I can see me too
No matter what I do
All day my Beloved
I feel you and only you
I yearn to meet you and
Hold you close so that
I can touch me too.

SOULMATE

Soulmate... is the one who
Connects you with your soul
Perceives the highest in you
And enables you to remain
Aligned with your Purpose
Soulmate... is the one who
Encourages you to stay on
The path and has the patience,
Courage and the commitment
To introduce you to yourself
Soulmate... is the one who
Lovingly brings your attention
To your light, to your shadow
And sets you off on a journey
Of discovery such that
You recognise your wholeness
Delight in your uniqueness
Revel in your magnificence
And joyfully become a channel
For divine grace to flow
Through you to touch and bless
All those who cross your path.

MIRACLE

Often I wonder my Beloved
Did I search for you or
Did you find me or maybe
Our paths just crossed
Often I wonder my Beloved
Which do I marvel more
The miracle of meeting you
Or the delight of knowing you.

SOLACE

And what name shall I
Call you my Beloved
My ancient spirit-friend
My assigned earth-angel
Mirror to my highest self
Or soulmate from eternity
For you transport me into
Ecstasy even in your absence
Just knowing that you are
But somewhere here on earth
Comforts me on dreary days
And lulls me into sweet sleep
Through long and lonely nights.

MERGING

As a faint sliver my Beloved
Of your cherished memories
Allow me to permeate
Your very presence
Like a soft blanket woven
With fragile strands
Of my longing adorned
Delicately with stardust
Permit me to surround
Your every sense.

DESIRE

And now my Beloved
The only desire I have left
Is to quietly breathe my last
In your arms listening
To the melody of your heart.

ALONE

Leave if you must
My Beloved, even when
I am alone with myself
I can feel the warmth
Of your heartbeat
And as I tune into the
Rhythm of your breath
I can hear the joyful
Songs in your eyes and
I can touch the soulful
Music in your dreams.

FLICKER

My love for you my Beloved
Is like the quiet flickering
Of the flame of a temple lamp
Lit in a tiny chalice of hope
Kept alive by the ache of longing
I cup my hands around
To protect its feeble glow
From the wanton breeze
Of the mundane so that
I remain immersed always
In your remembrance.

MEETING

Until you lived my Beloved
In my imagination, my Being
Was immersed in your presence
And suffused with your fragrance
But now that we met my Beloved
Even my dwelling reverberates
To the cadence of your heart
Light dances to your movements
While your voice stills the water
And the breeze carries your scent.

ECHO

When I listen to your voice
My Beloved I hear the echo
Of my words yet unspoken
When I hear your heartbeat
My Beloved I hear the swirl
Of my innermost thoughts
When I hold your hands
My Beloved I realise how
Holding me unconditionally
You led me to rejoice and to
Celebrate my own intensity
When I look into your eyes
My Beloved I see the trail
Of my journey from the
Intolerable torment of
Feeling desolate and invisible
To the unbearable ecstasy
Of feeling heard and of being
Seen, clearly in my own eyes.

THE VEIL

You must know my Beloved
That I have mastered the art
Of walking daintily but steady
In a world dimly visible through
The veil of my own making
Wearing my grief like a crown
Of glass delicate and shimmering
That enchants the world but
Not you for you have always
Looked beyond this alluring veil
Of dexterous grit and grace
And touched my deepest yearning
As you hold my face my Beloved
I can see in your limpid eyes
The melting of my crown of glass
Into warm droplets of tears.

REJUVENATION

How do you my Beloved always
Simply allow me to be until I see
My mind my shadow my universe
True and clear in your liquid eyes
For this moment and forever
Unsullied by the past the future
Untouched by fear or desire
So that my heart feels unburdened
My mind cleared my soul caressed
My spirit uplifted and I go forth
With deep conviction, rejuvenated
To pave my path at my own pace
And to create consciously my destiny.

HEALING

Do you know my Beloved
Your words kind and true
Cascade gently like a holy
Balm poured with love
On burning skin bruised
By my unconsciousness
Today I awoke my Beloved
Healed and radiant with
Renewed purpose, joyful
Like a bubbling stream.

SEEKING

First hide then seek then find
Darkness is seeking light
Ugliness is seeking witness
Confusion is seeking clarity
Beauty is seeking appreciation
Rejection is seeking validation
Compassion is seeking gratitude
The unseen is seeking visibility
The unconscious is seeking
Consciousness itself and
While seeking also is seeking
Its own fulfilment, the search
Must commence with awareness
Proceed with insight and come
To rest in Presence, where
Seeking ends and living begins.

PROMISE

Sometimes a kindred soul
Walks into your life like a
Gentle sunrise after a stormy
Night, soaking you in the
Warmth and glow, with the
Promise of a bright new day.

REFLECTION

Why do I so long for you
My precious Beloved
Because I see reflected
So clear and precise
In your smiling lotus eyes
The core of who I am and
The whole of who I am
It is because I see reflected
So clear and precise
In your twinkling lotus eyes
The essence of my being
The splendour of my doing
And the radiance of my love.

KINDRED SPIRIT

The one who honoured
A nameless timeless bond
The one who validated
A connection from beyond

The one who held steady
And mirrored my intensity
The one who helped me
Reclaim unbounded identity

The one who held space
Lovingly unconditionally
For me to be, to clearly see
My own infinite possibility

The one who is a balm
That always soothes a pain
The one who is an antidote
To my conditioned existence

The one who is a confidant
Revered guide and sweet friend
Tough teacher and teddy-bear
Delightfully 'role-d' into one.

NORTH STAR

But for you my Beloved
I wonder would I have
Ever thought of taking
A sip of Love Divine
But for you my Beloved
I wonder would I have
Ever learnt to tread
The path of Grace Divine.

AWARENESS

I am aware my Beloved
To see is to transcend
When I am aware that
I am aware such that I
Am aware of awareness
Itself, a pulsating melody
Coursing simultaneously
Through me and eternity
I am even more keenly
Aware my Beloved that
Every time I see you
I see me seeing you and you
Seeing me and in the seeing
Together seeing each other,
We see throbbing as one
Always, eternity you and me.

IMMERSION

My mind is always filled with
The image of your sparkling eyes
Whether I am awake or asleep
I only see your radiant face
I feel you in every breath
I hear you in every pulse
Touching my soul and spirit
Immersing deep my being in
The quiet contentment of love.

WITH ME

Whatever I do my Beloved
And Wherever I go
When I am with myself
There you are
No longer do I pine or wait
Anxiously to meet you
When I am with myself
There you are.

MAGIC MIRROR

In the sweetness of your smile
I remember my Beloved, I am
Beneficence and infinite grace am I
I am deliverance I am compassion
I am forgiveness I am magnanimity
I am acceptance and serenity am I

In the twinkle of your eyes
I realise my Beloved, I am
The candle and the flame am I
I am clairvoyance I am confidence
I am the daring dream-catcher and
Also the dream-actualiser am I

In the safety of your embrace
I perceive my Beloved,
I am Knowledge and Intuition am I
I am discovery I am creativity
I am channel I am the source
I am clarity and conviction am I

In my bitter-sweet longing
I discover my Beloved, I am
The surrender of tender bud
And the ripeness of fruit am I
I am also the sweetness of trust
And the soft caress of love am I

In the melody of your heartbeat
I discern my Beloved, I am the
Harbinger of hope and healing am I
The bearer of blessings and glad tidings
I am the radiance of unsullied truth
And the fullness of divine love am I

In the rhythm of your breath
I reckon my Beloved, I am
The learning and the growing am I
I am infinite I am indefinable
I am glory and I am splendour
I am wisdom and wonder am I.

LONGING

Beholding the Longing
For so long have I
Become engrossed
In the longing itself
That I cannot let go of
The familiarity of the ache
And the comfort of the pain
Then how can I expect
To receive what I long for
When I prevent Divine grace
Overflowing with abundance
From entering my inner space.

GRIEF

Grief that won't melt grief that won't thaw
Grief that won't cry grief that won't draw
Grief of seeing and of not seeing
Grief of being and of not being

Grief that won't sing grief that won't sleep
Grief that won't groom grief that won't eat
Grief so compelling you can only see doom
Grief so (full)filling that there is no room

Grief of doing and grief of not doing
Grief of having and grief of not having
Grief of hopelessly falling in love
So deep, that now there is the
Grief of losing one's known self, the
Grief of searching one's lost self and the
Grief of longing for one's true self

And then grief suddenly comes upon
Acceptance in a long embrace, like
Long-lost friends when they open
Their eyes they find themselves back
In the land of desires and dreams and
Plans and possibilities, to begin anew
The game of love and longing, to play
Yet again the game of grief and acceptance.

WHOLENESS

There is my Beloved an astute
Part of me that revels
In revealing only the best of my
Gilded mind and famed nobility
Intent upon impressing you
But then my Beloved there is
Another part of me also
Waiting quietly, yearning to lay
Utterly bare my heart and
Let you see the despair of my
Fragmented and barren soul
Because it knows you carry
In your smile and in your voice
In your twinkling lotus eyes
The warmth that will heal and
The touch that will restore
My spirit, and make me whole
And I also know my Beloved
That in your Presence
There is room enough for both
The golden diva of light and
The black deity of darkness
To rejoice together and celebrate
To embrace each other so I can
Become whole and complete.

RESTORATION

When I find my eyes cast
In dullness my Beloved
I remember the twinkle
In your eyes and restore
The shine of my own
When my voice goes
Missing my Beloved
I recall your tender words
And soon I begin to sing
The song of my own
When my heart goes
Silent my Beloved I tune
Into the melody of your
Heartbeat and connect with
The rhythm of my own
When my love feels lost
My Beloved I listen
Intently to the notes
In your breath and discover
The essence of my own.

DISTANCE

From a distance my Beloved
Beholds me softly, his eyes
Smiling gently draw me close
The tenderness on his face
And the warmth in his smile
Comfort me and pull me instantly
Out of the desolation around
My heart and the dark despair
Shrouding my lonely soul
Even from a distance ever
Immeasurable my Beloved
Can behold me thus and lull
Me into a slumber so sweet.

RECKONING

The Beloved is mesmerising
Leaves me spellbound but
The enchanted sweetness
Of beholding, of loving myself
Cascades ever so quietly
Over my soul and my spirit
And my entire being, like a
Gentle rain that washes
Away all dirt and leaves
The earth fresh and clean.

UNBROKEN

Do I love you my Beloved?
In the comfort of your
Gentle gaze, in the light of
Your clear presence I see
My unbroken worth and
I feel Precious whole and sane
When I say I love you
I'm merely seeking the
Clarity of your presence and
The warmth of your gaze
So I can experience again
My unbroken worth and feel
Whole precious and sane again
So I do not know if I love you
My Beloved but I do know I long
For the love deep within me
That only your presence ignites
And brings so radiantly alive.

PLAY

The Beloved plays with me
Hide and seek and hides
Again, seemingly invisible
Amongst the folds of his
Rose-coloured veil that
Is subtly tinted, with the
Colours of every season and
Hues of every bird and flower
Intent upon the rapturous
Melody of his heartbeat
My fingers move quietly
With trepidation, gently but
Fervently yearning to chance
Upon his handsome face.

SWING

The longing for you my Beloved
Awaits intently the cloudburst
Of soul-drenching love that leaves
Me radiant like the morning dew
After bidding goodbye begins the
Enchanting waft of memories of
Sweet togetherness, clashing with
Flaming winds of doubt and
Cool quenching drops of faith
Setting my heart on a wild swing
But unfailingly, in the magic of
Your tender embrace my Beloved
My questions melt along with me.

The warmth of your FRIENDSHIP nourishes my Being...

INITIATION

Strange are the ways
Of the Beloved he seemed
To have come only to open
Wide the doors of my heart
So that love can walk in with
Aplomb and make a home
Here now present and constant
Then love walked in as though
It owned my heart and as if
It belonged here since eternity.

PRIVILEGE

The many who surround you
My Beloved, know not the
Privilege of knowing you
The many who know you
My Beloved, have not the
Blessing of loving you
It is mine and mine alone
The privilege of beholding
You thus and the blessing of
Loving you so that my heart
Aches of loving you such that
My heart breaks leaving me
At once trembling and still
Breathless with anticipation
Lost in silent adoration and
Brimming over with gratitude
That you walk on this earth
So I can bear to be here too.

EVERYTHING

I ask me my Beloved who are you
They ask me my Beloved what are you
You are the ground and you are the flight
You are the bright day and the dark night
You are the thirst and the quenching as well
You are the teacher and the learning as well
You are the mirror and you are the reflection
You are contemplation and you are distraction
You are endurance and the release as well
You are the pulse and the pause as well
You are the echo and you are the silence
You are emptiness and you are resplendence
You are the longing and the redemption as well
You are the quest and the revelation as well
You are the inquiry and the insight also are you
You are the rhythm and the melody also are you
You are the journey and the destination as well
You are dissolution and the regeneration as well
Tell me my Beloved who are you not!
Tell them my Beloved what are you not!

PRECIOUSNESS

In the eyes of the Beloved
You see the clear reflection
Of your unconditional worth
And your unquestionable
Preciousness that immerses
You in sweet intoxication
You believe you have fallen
In love with the Beloved but
Soon you realise that you have
Hopelessly fallen in love
With yourself, and even as you
Long to connect with the Beloved
The Beloved reconnects you with your soul.

MELTING

Do you know my Beloved
That your love held me high
I could nimbly walk on water
And fly deftly in the sky
But my incessant longing
For your soothing embrace
Has melted the me I knew
Such that I have now
Become one with the fire
This ceaseless longing to be
In your arms my Beloved
Has taught me how to
Walk lightly on this earth
And to gracefully dance
While my heart is aflame.

WONDER

I will never cease
To wonder my Beloved
Whether it was my imagination
That wished you into being
Or was it my blazing intent
That nudged you into existence
I continue to wonder
Every moment my Beloved
Whether it was you
Who walked into my world
Or was it the Divine
Who willed you into mine.

UNFOLDING

Do you recall my Beloved
That before we descended
From the stars amongst whom
We lived loved and laughed
Onto this earth to learn lessons
So that our souls may expand

Do you recall my Beloved
That we'd agreed to meet
In the middle of our stories
When our souls would be
Well-worn but wiser from
Our many journeys immense

And when at last we met
On this earth my Beloved
Tell me if you saw your soul
In the twinkling of my eyes
Tell me if you heard your song
In the pounding of my heart
Tell me if you came alive
In the tremble of my embrace
Tell me if you felt at home
As you lay down in my arms

I have whispered to you
Unabashedly time and again
How your pristine presence
Enchants my very existence
I have whispered to you
Unabashedly time and again
How your magnanimous spirit
Envelopes my soul with grace
I have whispered to you
Unabashedly time and again
It is your love immeasurable
That I now carry as my name.

EPILOGUE

"Over and over again, there is the possibility of coming home just by noticing, and caring about what we find." — **Joan Sutherland**

The path of love usually follows the well-worn steps of attraction, courtship, exclusive engagement, and/or co-habitation, eventually leading to a 'committed relationship' or marriage, with an ardent hope for the 'happily ever after.' However, given who broke through the fortress around my heart and set it aflutter, it was neither possible nor appealing, for either of us to tread this common path.

As a psychotherapist in private practice, for well over two decades, working mostly with painful relationship issues of married and dating couples, I had grown somewhat weary with countless stories of 'failed love.' Of late, the focus of my practice had organically evolved, from helping distressed couples to understand each other and restore love, to helping warring partners to redeem their relationship, by seeing and using the conflict/betrayal as a path to self-discovery and personal growth.

My own experience of being in a long-suffering marriage added to my disdain about what humans did or failed to do, while claiming to be in love. Although my marriage had been over for the better part of the 20 years I was in it, it was only less than a year since my divorce had come through. I was completely focused on my own recovery: renting a new place to live, going for healing sessions, raising my two little girls, seeing clients, offering workshops, figuring out my finances, and getting my fragmented life back together. **I was certainly not 'looking for love.'**

At a time, when I was fully convinced that my inner space was permanently parched, love thundered upon it suddenly, unbidden and unannounced, along with the monsoon that year, thanks to an extraordinary man. A man I had never met, a man far removed from my world, a man who was fully occupied living his own life on a different continent, a man who didn't even know that I existed on this planet.

I had chanced upon his picture and was transfixed by his eyes. While my heart pounded wildly, I felt flushed with an uncanny sweetness and warmth. I felt I had come home to an ancient kindred soul whom I had known forever, and from whom I had been accidentally separated. I was seized by a baffling need to 'update' him about my life, as though I owed him a report on how I had fared so far in the journey apart from him. **The tremendous sense of familiarity and connection I felt with him completely erased the incredulity of the situation.** On the contrary, I felt compelled by a persistent desire to somehow get in touch with him.

As I was to soon discover, he was married, and utterly devoted to his beautiful family. He was also married to his purpose and passionately dedicated to his vision. I must admit that this has caused me to feel at once, a wrenching mix of immense admiration and utter desolation, even to this day. Admiration, to have come across in flesh and blood, an excruciatingly precise match of my highest, grandest vision of a life-partner. And desolation, at the obvious unattainability of it. This vision that I had nurtured from my teenage years, was not merely about a romantic relationship or a happy married life. **It was about having someone with shared values and purpose, to live and to work with. To accomplish together something grand and extraordinary, something of lasting value to the world. It was about exploring together a lifetime of deep communion.**

In the weeks that followed, I felt inexorably captive in the grip of an emotional vortex. My world seemed shrouded in beatific luminosity. I floated through my routine of work and domesticity, with a heart full of causeless joy. There was a lightness in my step and a lilt in my voice. The twinkle that had gone missing from my eyes for years, returned. I was acutely aware of, and highly embarrassed by, the unnerving vulnerability I felt at the mere thought of him – something I had never experienced with anyone else. It was delicious and disorienting at the same time. I felt infused by his energy and enveloped in his aura, every waking moment. I mused if this is how Meera Bai felt about Shri Krishna, or Rumi felt towards Shams. **I wondered if this is how it felt when Divine grace descended upon an unsuspecting mortal.**

Uncharacteristically, I decided to reach out to him. We interacted via email, text messages, and occasional phone calls. Despite these sporadic exchanges, I discerned in him attributes that I deeply valued and cherished. I saw in him the light of clear presence. A deep respect for, and connection to, self and others. Formidable strength of mind. Passion for action. Consistent self-awareness. Honour for his word. Vibrant energy. Matter-of-fact transparency and earnestness. Enormous patience. Sparkling intelligence. Wide-eyed curiosity. Persistent exploration of the inner and outer worlds.

Uncommon humility, alongside an unapologetic knowing of his own significance and place in the world. Conviction of consciously embraced values. Unusual care and concern for the well-being of others. A wry sense of humor. Clarity of purpose. Tremendous courage. Uncompromising integrity and ethics. Amazing resourcefulness. Spontaneous creativity and playfulness. Eloquent expression of inner experiences and outer observations. Natural tenderness. Openness by default, almost to a fault. Childlike innocence. And an extraordinarily large heart.

Basically, someone who was alive and kicking, fully engaged with this world, but somehow untouched by it.

Clearly, I had begun to idealise and idolise him. The precision of his intellect, softened by the warmth in his voice, entranced me like a magic mirror. For the very first time in my entire life, I felt accurately heard and understood for who I was. I felt seen for who I was yet to be and become. I felt deeply supported by the natural blend of his unapologetic masculinity and innate femininity. I felt held, like a woman needs and wants to be held – with respect, tenderness and adoration. I felt honoured by his regard and attention. I felt healed of a lifetime of shame, sorrow and grief. I felt real, good and beautiful. I felt free to be fully me – scared child, skilled therapist, mischievous girl, brilliant teacher, loving mother, wise crone, full woman, all at once. I felt recognised and rewarded by the Almighty for whatever good I had done in the world. Even though it was an infrequent 'digital dialogue' across the oceans, the communion I experienced with him can only be described as numinous.

At first, I disbelieved this entire experience even as it was unfolding. I dismissed it as infatuation, denied its impact even to myself, and was determined not to make any meanings out of it. It was clear that he cared a great deal about me, but he probably engaged with any human being in the same way – with presence, respect and care. Much as I wanted to believe that I was special to him, he never spoke or behaved in a way that fuelled my hope or raised my expectations. While he was certainly not available for a relationship, in the usual sense of the word, **I found him to be available to me in a way that no other person in my life had ever cared to be**. And I had no intention of complicating our respective lives by 'expressing my feelings.'

Inevitably, this self-imposed refusal to acknowledge or articulate my truth morphed into an unbearably intense longing – a feeling I had only heard and read about, but never ever experienced. **Longing can be bittersweet, bewildering, and intoxicating – a strange blend of fullness and emptiness, comfort and anxiety, contentment and deprivation, all at once.** Longing feeds on itself and becomes addictive. Over a period, longing interferes with your ability to be present, almost paralyses you, and renders you unproductive. It can also lead to persistent feelings of self-doubt and despair.

As the longing became intolerable, I began to severely judge and question my feelings themselves: How can you feel this way about a married man? How can you feel so intensely for someone you've never met? Why would you spend so much of your energy over something that has no hope of going anywhere? Unless you are willing to break your own rules and betray your own values? But then, if you claim to feel so deeply and strongly, how can it be inappropriate to let him know about it? Should you not give it a fighting chance? Can't believe you are such a prude. You are just stupid. No, you are a coward. Actually, you just don't know what you want in life... My ego was having a go at me ruthlessly. **I was completely exhausted from relentlessly pining for him and simultaneously rebuking myself.**

I did not have a clear or steady answer to any of these questions, mainly due to my own ambivalence about getting involved in any close relationship, leave alone an intimate relationship with a married man. Due to the prolonged emotional turmoil I had to deal with in my marriage, I felt completely spent. I seriously doubted if I had anything meaningful left to give to anyone, leave alone this precious human being. While I deeply cherished the natural bond I felt with him, I also saw it as an emotional-spiritual attachment that was intense but perhaps one-sided. And I absolutely did not want to jeopardise the inexplicable friendship that had evolved between us. **The dilemma thus was not about whether I** *could/should* **reveal to him the state of my heart. The dilemma was about how I should deal with it without sinking into a damning, dark despair.**

Of the many things I had experienced with this remarkable man was the highest order of empathy – the diligent art and meticulous science of listening deeply, as a witness, without adding or removing anything from the situation, holding a steady intent for the highest outcome, and facilitating the emergence of a new perspective, insight or solution. While the practice of empathy is the cornerstone of my entire career, I have often been either stingy or forgetful in extending it to myself, especially when I am most in need of it.

One fine day, I asked myself: If I share this with him as a 'problem', how would he respond? And the instant, matter-of-fact answer came: undoubtedly, with utmost respect, openness, curiosity, concern, and no judgment! So, was it possible for me to extend that generosity to myself? Was I ready to hold the space for my own heart? **Instead of seeing the situation as futile, could I look at how the experience had touched and enriched me?** Instead of ruing what was not feasible, could I pay attention to what was available?

In permitting myself to feel whatever I was feeling, without shame or guilt, I began to feel comforted by the very experience that I was resisting so hard and long. Once I stopped fighting with my own emotions, I could relax into them and relish their richness and depth. As I allowed myself to fully experience how I was enamoured by this unusual encounter, I felt greatly consoled. Every time I felt a wave of longing (which on some days, was as frequent as my breathing!), instead of distracting or berating myself, I tried to express it in writing, colouring, craft, decoration and cooking. And to my surprise and delight, poetic verse, prose, sketches, beautiful mandalas, interesting recipes, memes, quotes and insights emerged and flowed effortlessly. The artwork and poetry became a source of joy, an immersive and enriching 'date with myself.' **The poems became a ceaseless love-song that I wrote for and sang to him, and also to myself. In the process, I became my own Beloved.**

Gradually, I began to feel an abiding sense of gratitude for this exquisite experience, of being bowled over by a stranger who matter-of-factly meets your deepest need to 'Be-loved' and gives you the gift of unconditional friendship. I now feel specially privileged to be the recipient of this uncanny stroke of Grace. In fact, I am happy that this relationship did not have the opportunity to follow the usual path – while that might have had its own joys and learnings, I wonder if it would have led me to recognise my inherent wholeness, or discover my intrinsic capacity for unconditional love in this unusual way.

Over time, this precious friendship has grown and deepened. To this day, his steadfast presence in my life continues to nourish my heart, replenish my being, nurture my soul and brighten my world. I continue to nurse a silent hope that in the future, near or far, in some way, we both might come together to work on a book or a project or some pioneering idea, born out of our mutually shared values, that would leave a deep and lasting impact on the world, well before we take leave of it.

While I have always been a die-hard romantic, I am also an equally strong rationalist. I used to be fascinated by the idea of soulmates/twinflames, yet the sceptic in me always took it with a pinch of salt. After this surreal experience, however, I am more than convinced that it is possible for two human beings, despite being geographically and otherwise very far removed from each other's worlds, to feel such an intricate and unquestionable bond with each other. While they may exist in separate bodies, they probably do belong to one soul!

I have now come to believe that the inner journey of the heart is no less perilous and heroic than the outer journey of the hero/heroine. It calls for the same kind of courage to slay the dragons of self-doubt, selfishness and hopelessness. It calls for the same kind of commitment to stay the path and not turn your back to the challenge, with excuses and rationalisations. It calls for the same kind of care for, and adherence to, your own values and principles. It also calls for a keen awareness of the other's boundary and space, along with respect and gratitude for their ability and willingness to walk this path with you, in the manner and to the extent they can, because they are in no way obliged to.

This is an adventure of the heart, for the heart, and by the heart. It demands a rare bravado, for it entails venturing into uncharted territory with nothing but your experiential truth as the roadmap. **But having taken it, I can vouch that it is worth every agony, for you return from it transformed into a version of yourself that you would have never imagined possible**. Here's a gist of what I learned from this intrepid journey:

1. The real value of a desire is not its attainment, but in what one can become while pursuing it. The value of love is not only in its reciprocation, but also in the priceless gift of self-discovery, if you allow yourself to experience it without insisting on a particular outcome.

2. You cannot will yourself to let go of longing. When you concede to embrace it fully, longing releases its grip on you.

3. Loneliness comes not from having an unmet need for companionship, but from telling yourself that the need is unimportant, unnecessary or unacceptable.

4. Held close for long enough, gently and firmly, longing expands the heart, and transforms itself into love for oneself without judgment, and love for the other without clinging.

5. It is splendid when you see your soul reflected in the eyes of another. But it is transformational when you can see your soul's reflection in your own eyes.

6. Love heals and nourishes the one who loves, infinitely more than the one who is loved.

7. From hoping to feel worthy only if/when loved by another, to discovering and exercising your own capacity to love unconditionally – this, is the real Journey of the Heart!

Love, I believe, is incredibly powerful, like 'cosmic clay,' the star- stuff that the Universe is made of. Love has the same attributes too – it is unlimited and pliable – ready and willing to take on the shape and form that YOU want it take! **When you handle love with reverence and wonder, it infuses your life with amazing creativity and fulfilment.**

I also believe that it is not you who picked this book, rather it is this book that has found you, at the exact time in your life that you most need it! May you feel inspired to walk this inner path, with infinitely rich treasures, rather than the outer path, which very often, results in heart-break and anguish, for all concerned. **May your heart be open and may your inner-space be still. May you hear the song loud and clear, When The Beloved Calls.**

May you have the courage to journey and find your Beloved within. May you dance together into eternity. May you radiate love always!

Sujata Ameya
Hyderabad, India
1st January, 2019